This book belongs to:

_____

My Personal Information

Name: _____

Address: _____

_____

_____

Phone: _____
Email: _____

In case of emergency please notify:

Name: _____

Address: _____

_____

_____

Phone: _____
Email: _____

Travel Details

Cruise Destination: _____

Cruise Line: _____

Departing From: _____

Date: _____

Traveling to ship via: _____

Time of Departure: _____

Flight: _____ Gate: _____

Time of Arrival: _____

Notes:

_____

_____

_____

_____

_____

_____

_____

Travel Journal,
Cruise Log,
Pocketbook Edition

Created by

Denis and Deanne Swenson

Travel Journals, Volume 9---First Edition
ISBN-10: 1515067505
ISBN-13: 978-1515067504

Daily Cruise Log

Date: _____ Location: _____

Destination Port: _____

Weather: _____

Route: _____

Miles Traveled: _____

Shore Excursions:

_____

_____

_____

_____

_____

Items of Interest:

_____

_____

_____

_____

_____

_____

_____

_____

_____

_____

_____

Expenditures:

_____

_____

_____

_____

_____

_____

Daily Cruise Log

Date: _____ Location: _____

Destination Port: _____

Weather: _____

Route: _____

Miles Traveled: _____

Shore Excursions:

_____

_____

_____

_____

_____

Items of Interest:

_____

_____

_____

_____

_____

_____

_____

_____

_____

_____

Expenditures:

_____

_____

_____

_____

_____

_____

Daily Cruise Log

Date: _____ Location: _____

Destination Port: _____

Weather: _____

Route: _____

Miles Traveled: _____

Shore Excursions:

_____

_____

_____

_____

_____

Items of Interest:

_____

_____

_____

_____

_____

_____

_____

_____

_____

_____

_____

Expenditures:

_____

_____

_____

_____

_____

_____

Daily Cruise Log

Date: _____ Location: _____

Destination Port: _____

Weather: _____

Route: _____

Miles Traveled: _____

Shore Excursions:

_____

_____

_____

_____

_____

Items of Interest:

_____

_____

_____

_____

_____

_____

_____

_____

_____

_____

Expenditures:

_____

_____

_____

_____

_____

_____

Daily Cruise Log

Date: _____ Location: _____

Destination Port: _____

Weather: _____

Route: _____

Miles Traveled: _____

Shore Excursions:

_____

_____

_____

_____

_____

Items of Interest:

_____

_____

_____

_____

_____

_____

_____

_____

_____

_____

_____

Expenditures:

_____

_____

_____

_____

_____

_____

Daily Cruise Log

Date: _____ Location: _____

Destination Port: _____

Weather: _____

Route: _____

Miles Traveled: _____

Shore Excursions:

_____

_____

_____

_____

_____

Items of Interest:

_____

_____

_____

_____

_____

_____

_____

_____

_____

_____

Expenditures:

_____

_____

_____

_____

_____

_____

Daily Cruise Log

Date: _____ Location: _____

Destination Port: _____

Weather: _____

Route: _____

Miles Traveled: _____

Shore Excursions:

_____

_____

_____

_____

_____

Items of Interest:

_____

_____

_____

_____

_____

_____

_____

_____

_____

_____

_____

Expenditures:

_____

_____

_____

_____

_____

_____

Daily Cruise Log

Date: _____ Location: _____

Destination Port: _____

Weather: _____

Route: _____

Miles Traveled: _____

Shore Excursions:

_____

_____

_____

_____

_____

Items of Interest:

_____

_____

_____

_____

_____

_____

_____

_____

_____

_____

Expenditures:

_____

_____

_____

_____

_____

_____

Daily Cruise Log

Date: _____ Location: _____

Destination Port: _____

Weather: _____

Route: _____

Miles Traveled: _____

Shore Excursions:

_____
_____
_____
_____
_____

Items of Interest:

_____
_____
_____
_____
_____
_____
_____
_____
_____
_____
_____

Expenditures:

_____
_____
_____
_____
_____
_____

Daily Cruise Log

Date: _____ Location: _____

Destination Port: _____

Weather: _____

Route: _____

Miles Traveled: _____

Shore Excursions:

_____

_____

_____

_____

_____

Items of Interest:

_____

_____

_____

_____

_____

_____

_____

_____

_____

_____

_____

Expenditures:

_____

_____

_____

_____

_____

_____

Daily Cruise Log

Date: _____ Location: _____

Destination Port: _____

Weather: _____

Route: _____

Miles Traveled: _____

Shore Excursions:

_____

_____

_____

_____

_____

Items of Interest:

_____

_____

_____

_____

_____

_____

_____

_____

_____

_____

_____

Expenditures:

_____

_____

_____

_____

_____

_____

Daily Cruise Log

Date: _____ Location: _____

Destination Port: _____

Weather: _____

Route: _____

Miles Traveled: _____

Shore Excursions:

_____

_____

_____

_____

_____

Items of Interest:

_____

_____

_____

_____

_____

_____

_____

_____

_____

_____

Expenditures:

_____

_____

_____

_____

_____

_____

Daily Cruise Log

Date: _____ Location: _____

Destination Port: _____

Weather: _____

Route: _____

Miles Traveled: _____

Shore Excursions:

_____

_____

_____

_____

_____

Items of Interest:

_____

_____

_____

_____

_____

_____

_____

_____

_____

_____

_____

Expenditures:

_____

_____

_____

_____

_____

_____

Daily Cruise Log

Date: _____ Location: _____

Destination Port: _____

Weather: _____

Route: _____

Miles Traveled: _____

Shore Excursions:

_____

_____

_____

_____

_____

Items of Interest:

_____

_____

_____

_____

_____

_____

_____

_____

_____

_____

Expenditures:

_____

_____

_____

_____

_____

_____

Daily Cruise Log

Date: _____ Location: _____

Destination Port: _____

Weather: _____

Route: _____

Miles Traveled: _____

Shore Excursions:

_____

_____

_____

_____

_____

Items of Interest:

_____

_____

_____

_____

_____

_____

_____

_____

_____

_____

_____

Expenditures:

_____

_____

_____

_____

_____

_____

Daily Cruise Log

Date: _____ Location: _____

Destination Port: _____

Weather: _____

Route: _____

Miles Traveled: _____

Shore Excursions:

_____
_____
_____
_____
_____

Items of Interest:

_____
_____
_____
_____
_____
_____
_____
_____
_____
_____
_____

Expenditures:

_____
_____
_____
_____
_____
_____

Daily Cruise Log

Date: _____ Location: _____

Destination Port: _____

Weather: _____

Route: _____

Miles Traveled: _____

Shore Excursions:

_____

_____

_____

_____

_____

Items of Interest:

_____

_____

_____

_____

_____

_____

_____

_____

_____

_____

_____

Expenditures:

_____

_____

_____

_____

_____

_____

Daily Cruise Log

Date: _____ Location: _____

Destination Port: _____

Weather: _____

Route: _____

Miles Traveled: _____

Shore Excursions:

_____

_____

_____

_____

_____

Items of Interest:

_____

_____

_____

_____

_____

_____

_____

_____

_____

_____

_____

Expenditures:

_____

_____

_____

_____

_____

_____

Daily Cruise Log

Date: _____ Location: _____

Destination Port: _____

Weather: _____

Route: _____

Miles Traveled: _____

Shore Excursions:

_____

_____

_____

_____

_____

Items of Interest:

_____

_____

_____

_____

_____

_____

_____

_____

_____

_____

Expenditures:

_____

_____

_____

_____

_____

_____

Daily Cruise Log

Date: _____ Location: _____

Destination Port: _____

Weather: _____

Route: _____

Miles Traveled: _____

Shore Excursions:

_____

_____

_____

_____

_____

Items of Interest:

_____

_____

_____

_____

_____

_____

_____

_____

_____

_____

Expenditures:

_____

_____

_____

_____

_____

_____

Daily Cruise Log

Date: _____ Location: _____

Destination Port: _____

Weather: _____

Route: _____

Miles Traveled: _____

Shore Excursions:

_____
_____
_____
_____
_____

Items of Interest:

_____
_____
_____
_____
_____
_____
_____
_____
_____
_____
_____

Expenditures:

_____
_____
_____
_____
_____
_____

Daily Cruise Log

Date: _____ Location: _____

Destination Port: _____

Weather: _____

Route: _____

Miles Traveled: _____

Shore Excursions:

_____

_____

_____

_____

_____

Items of Interest:

_____

_____

_____

_____

_____

_____

_____

_____

_____

_____

Expenditures:

_____

_____

_____

_____

_____

_____

Daily Cruise Log

Date: _____ Location: _____

Destination Port: _____

Weather: _____

Route: _____

Miles Traveled: _____

Shore Excursions:

_____

_____

_____

_____

_____

Items of Interest:

_____

_____

_____

_____

_____

_____

_____

_____

_____

_____

Expenditures:

_____

_____

_____

_____

_____

_____

Daily Cruise Log

Date: _____ Location: _____

Destination Port: _____

Weather: _____

Route: _____

Miles Traveled: _____

Shore Excursions:

_____
_____
_____
_____
_____

Items of Interest:

_____
_____
_____
_____
_____
_____
_____
_____
_____
_____
_____

Expenditures:

_____
_____
_____
_____
_____
_____

Daily Cruise Log

Date: _____ Location: _____

Destination Port: _____

Weather: _____

Route: _____

Miles Traveled: _____

Shore Excursions:

_____

_____

_____

_____

_____

Items of Interest:

_____

_____

_____

_____

_____

_____

_____

_____

_____

_____

Expenditures:

_____

_____

_____

_____

_____

_____

Daily Cruise Log

Date: _____ Location: _____

Destination Port: _____

Weather: _____

Route: _____

Miles Traveled: _____

Shore Excursions:

_____

_____

_____

_____

_____

Items of Interest:

_____

_____

_____

_____

_____

_____

_____

_____

_____

_____

Expenditures:

_____

_____

_____

_____

_____

_____

Daily Cruise Log

Date: _____ Location: _____

Destination Port: _____

Weather: _____

Route: _____

Miles Traveled: _____

Shore Excursions:

_____

_____

_____

_____

_____

Items of Interest:

_____

_____

_____

_____

_____

_____

_____

_____

_____

_____

_____

Expenditures:

_____

_____

_____

_____

_____

_____

Daily Cruise Log

Date: _____ Location: _____

Destination Port: _____

Weather: _____

Route: _____

Miles Traveled: _____

Shore Excursions:

_____

_____

_____

_____

_____

Items of Interest:

_____

_____

_____

_____

_____

_____

_____

_____

_____

_____

Expenditures:

_____

_____

_____

_____

_____

_____

Daily Cruise Log

Date: _____ Location: _____

Destination Port: _____

Weather: _____

Route: _____

Miles Traveled: _____

Shore Excursions:

_____

_____

_____

_____

_____

Items of Interest:

_____

_____

_____

_____

_____

_____

_____

_____

_____

_____

_____

Expenditures:

_____

_____

_____

_____

_____

_____

Daily Cruise Log

Date: _____ Location: _____

Destination Port: _____

Weather: _____

Route: _____

Miles Traveled: _____

Shore Excursions:

_____
_____
_____
_____
_____

Items of Interest:

_____
_____
_____
_____
_____
_____
_____
_____
_____
_____
_____

Expenditures:

_____
_____
_____
_____
_____
_____

Daily Cruise Log

Date: _____ Location: _____

Destination Port: _____

Weather: _____

Route: _____

Miles Traveled: _____

Shore Excursions:

_____
_____
_____
_____
_____

Items of Interest:

_____
_____
_____
_____
_____
_____
_____
_____
_____
_____
_____

Expenditures:

_____
_____
_____
_____
_____
_____

Daily Cruise Log

Date: _____ Location: _____

Destination Port: _____

Weather: _____

Route: _____

Miles Traveled: _____

Shore Excursions:

_____

_____

_____

_____

_____

Items of Interest:

_____

_____

_____

_____

_____

_____

_____

_____

_____

_____

Expenditures:

_____

_____

_____

_____

_____

_____

Daily Cruise Log

Date: _____ Location: _____

Destination Port: _____

Weather: _____

Route: _____

Miles Traveled: _____

Shore Excursions:

_____
_____
_____
_____
_____

Items of Interest:

_____
_____
_____
_____
_____
_____
_____
_____
_____
_____
_____

Expenditures:

_____
_____
_____
_____
_____
_____

Daily Cruise Log

Date: _____ Location: _____

Destination Port: _____

Weather: _____

Route: _____

Miles Traveled: _____

Shore Excursions:

_____

_____

_____

_____

_____

Items of Interest:

_____

_____

_____

_____

_____

_____

_____

_____

_____

_____

Expenditures:

_____

_____

_____

_____

_____

_____

Daily Cruise Log

Date: _____ Location: _____

Destination Port: _____

Weather: _____

Route: _____

Miles Traveled: _____

Shore Excursions:

_____

_____

_____

_____

_____

Items of Interest:

_____

_____

_____

_____

_____

_____

_____

_____

_____

_____

Expenditures:

_____

_____

_____

_____

_____

_____

Daily Cruise Log

Date: _____ Location: _____

Destination Port: _____

Weather: _____

Route: _____

Miles Traveled: _____

Shore Excursions:

_____

_____

_____

_____

_____

Items of Interest:

_____

_____

_____

_____

_____

_____

_____

_____

_____

_____

Expenditures:

_____

_____

_____

_____

_____

_____

Daily Cruise Log

Date: _____ Location: _____

Destination Port: _____

Weather: _____

Route: _____

Miles Traveled: _____

Shore Excursions:

_____

_____

_____

_____

_____

Items of Interest:

_____

_____

_____

_____

_____

_____

_____

_____

_____

_____

Expenditures:

_____

_____

_____

_____

_____

_____

Daily Cruise Log

Date: _____ Location: _____

Destination Port: _____

Weather: _____

Route: _____

Miles Traveled: _____

Shore Excursions:

_____

_____

_____

_____

_____

Items of Interest:

_____

_____

_____

_____

_____

_____

_____

_____

_____

_____

Expenditures:

_____

_____

_____

_____

_____

_____

Daily Cruise Log

Date: _____ Location: _____

Destination Port: _____

Weather: _____

Route: _____

Miles Traveled: _____

Shore Excursions:

_____

_____

_____

_____

_____

Items of Interest:

_____

_____

_____

_____

_____

_____

_____

_____

_____

_____

_____

Expenditures:

_____

_____

_____

_____

_____

_____

Daily Cruise Log

Date: _____ Location: _____

Destination Port: _____

Weather: _____

Route: _____

Miles Traveled: _____

Shore Excursions:

_____

_____

_____

_____

_____

Items of Interest:

_____

_____

_____

_____

_____

_____

_____

_____

_____

_____

_____

Expenditures:

_____

_____

_____

_____

_____

_____

Daily Cruise Log

Date: _____ Location: _____

Destination Port: _____

Weather: _____

Route: _____

Miles Traveled: _____

Shore Excursions:

_____

_____

_____

_____

_____

Items of Interest:

_____

_____

_____

_____

_____

_____

_____

_____

_____

_____

_____

Expenditures:

_____

_____

_____

_____

_____

_____

Daily Cruise Log

Date: _____ Location: _____

Destination Port: _____

Weather: _____

Route: _____

Miles Traveled: _____

Shore Excursions:

_____

_____

_____

_____

_____

Items of Interest:

_____

_____

_____

_____

_____

_____

_____

_____

_____

_____

Expenditures:

_____

_____

_____

_____

_____

_____

Daily Cruise Log

Date: _____ Location: _____

Destination Port: _____

Weather: _____

Route: _____

Miles Traveled: _____

Shore Excursions:

_____

_____

_____

_____

_____

Items of Interest:

_____

_____

_____

_____

_____

_____

_____

_____

_____

_____

Expenditures:

_____

_____

_____

_____

_____

_____

Daily Cruise Log

Date: _____ Location: _____

Destination Port: _____

Weather: _____

Route: _____

Miles Traveled: _____

Shore Excursions:

_____

_____

_____

_____

_____

Items of Interest:

_____

_____

_____

_____

_____

_____

_____

_____

_____

_____

_____

Expenditures:

_____

_____

_____

_____

_____

_____

Daily Cruise Log

Date: _____ Location: _____

Destination Port: _____

Weather: _____

Route: _____

Miles Traveled: _____

Shore Excursions:

_____

_____

_____

_____

_____

Items of Interest:

_____

_____

_____

_____

_____

_____

_____

_____

_____

_____

_____

Expenditures:

_____

_____

_____

_____

_____

_____

Daily Cruise Log

Date: _____ Location: _____

Destination Port: _____

Weather: _____

Route: _____

Miles Traveled: _____

Shore Excursions:

_____

_____

_____

_____

_____

Items of Interest:

_____

_____

_____

_____

_____

_____

_____

_____

_____

_____

Expenditures:

_____

_____

_____

_____

_____

_____

Daily Cruise Log

Date: _____ Location: _____

Destination Port: _____

Weather: _____

Route: _____

Miles Traveled: _____

Shore Excursions:

_____

_____

_____

_____

_____

Items of Interest:

_____

_____

_____

_____

_____

_____

_____

_____

_____

_____

_____

Expenditures:

_____

_____

_____

_____

_____

_____

Daily Cruise Log

Date: _____ Location: _____

Destination Port: _____

Weather: _____

Route: _____

Miles Traveled: _____

Shore Excursions:

_____

_____

_____

_____

_____

Items of Interest:

_____

_____

_____

_____

_____

_____

_____

_____

_____

_____

Expenditures:

_____

_____

_____

_____

_____

_____

Daily Cruise Log

Date: _____ Location: _____

Destination Port: _____

Weather: _____

Route: _____

Miles Traveled: _____

Shore Excursions:

_____

_____

_____

_____

_____

Items of Interest:

_____

_____

_____

_____

_____

_____

_____

_____

_____

_____

Expenditures:

_____

_____

_____

_____

_____

_____

Daily Cruise Log

Date: _____ Location: _____

Destination Port: _____

Weather: _____

Route: _____

Miles Traveled: _____

Shore Excursions:

_____

_____

_____

_____

_____

Items of Interest:

_____

_____

_____

_____

_____

_____

_____

_____

_____

_____

Expenditures:

_____

_____

_____

_____

_____

_____

Daily Cruise Log

Date: _____ Location: _____

Destination Port: _____

Weather: _____

Route: _____

Miles Traveled: _____

Shore Excursions:

_____

_____

_____

_____

_____

Items of Interest:

_____

_____

_____

_____

_____

_____

_____

_____

_____

_____

Expenditures:

_____

_____

_____

_____

_____

_____

Daily Cruise Log

Date: _____ Location: _____

Destination Port: _____

Weather: _____

Route: _____

Miles Traveled: _____

Shore Excursions:

_____

_____

_____

_____

_____

Items of Interest:

_____

_____

_____

_____

_____

_____

_____

_____

_____

_____

Expenditures:

_____

_____

_____

_____

_____

_____

Daily Cruise Log

Date: _____ Location: _____

Destination Port: _____

Weather: _____

Route: _____

Miles Traveled: _____

Shore Excursions:

_____

_____

_____

_____

_____

Items of Interest:

_____

_____

_____

_____

_____

_____

_____

_____

_____

_____

_____

Expenditures:

_____

_____

_____

_____

_____

_____

Daily Cruise Log

Date: _____ Location: _____

Destination Port: _____

Weather: _____

Route: _____

Miles Traveled: _____

Shore Excursions:

_____
_____
_____
_____
_____

Items of Interest:

_____
_____
_____
_____
_____
_____
_____
_____
_____
_____
_____

Expenditures:

_____
_____
_____
_____
_____
_____

Daily Cruise Log

Date: _____ Location: _____

Destination Port: _____

Weather: _____

Route: _____

Miles Traveled: _____

Shore Excursions:

_____

_____

_____

_____

_____

Items of Interest:

_____

_____

_____

_____

_____

_____

_____

_____

_____

_____

Expenditures:

_____

_____

_____

_____

_____

_____

Daily Cruise Log

Date: _____ Location: _____

Destination Port: _____

Weather: _____

Route: _____

Miles Traveled: _____

Shore Excursions:

_____

_____

_____

_____

_____

Items of Interest:

_____

_____

_____

_____

_____

_____

_____

_____

_____

_____

_____

Expenditures:

_____

_____

_____

_____

_____

_____

Daily Cruise Log

Date: _____ Location: _____

Destination Port: _____

Weather: _____

Route: _____

Miles Traveled: _____

Shore Excursions:

_____

_____

_____

_____

_____

Items of Interest:

_____

_____

_____

_____

_____

_____

_____

_____

_____

_____

Expenditures:

_____

_____

_____

_____

_____

_____

Daily Cruise Log

Date: _____ Location: _____

Destination Port: _____

Weather: _____

Route: _____

Miles Traveled: _____

Shore Excursions:

_____

_____

_____

_____

_____

Items of Interest:

_____

_____

_____

_____

_____

_____

_____

_____

_____

_____

Expenditures:

_____

_____

_____

_____

_____

_____

Daily Cruise Log

Date: _____ Location: _____

Destination Port: _____

Weather: _____

Route: _____

Miles Traveled: _____

Shore Excursions:

_____

_____

_____

_____

_____

Items of Interest:

_____

_____

_____

_____

_____

_____

_____

_____

_____

_____

_____

Expenditures:

_____

_____

_____

_____

_____

_____

Daily Cruise Log

Date: _____ Location: _____

Destination Port: _____

Weather: _____

Route: _____

Miles Traveled: _____

Shore Excursions:

_____

_____

_____

_____

_____

Items of Interest:

_____

_____

_____

_____

_____

_____

_____

_____

_____

_____

_____

Expenditures:

_____

_____

_____

_____

_____

_____

Daily Cruise Log

Date: _____ Location: _____

Destination Port: _____

Weather: _____

Route: _____

Miles Traveled: _____

Shore Excursions:

_____

_____

_____

_____

_____

Items of Interest:

_____

_____

_____

_____

_____

_____

_____

_____

_____

_____

Expenditures:

_____

_____

_____

_____

_____

_____

Daily Cruise Log

Date: _____ Location: _____

Destination Port: _____

Weather: _____

Route: _____

Miles Traveled: _____

Shore Excursions:

_____

_____

_____

_____

_____

Items of Interest:

_____

_____

_____

_____

_____

_____

_____

_____

_____

_____

_____

Expenditures:

_____

_____

_____

_____

_____

_____

Daily Cruise Log

Date: _____ Location: _____

Destination Port: _____

Weather: _____

Route: _____

Miles Traveled: _____

Shore Excursions:

_____
_____
_____
_____
_____

Items of Interest:

_____
_____
_____
_____
_____
_____
_____
_____
_____
_____
_____

Expenditures:

_____
_____
_____
_____
_____
_____

Daily Cruise Log

Date: _____ Location: _____

Destination Port: _____

Weather: _____

Route: _____

Miles Traveled: _____

Shore Excursions:

_____
_____
_____
_____
_____

Items of Interest:

_____
_____
_____
_____
_____
_____
_____
_____
_____
_____
_____

Expenditures:

_____
_____
_____
_____
_____
_____

Daily Cruise Log

Date: _____ Location: _____

Destination Port: _____

Weather: _____

Route: _____

Miles Traveled: _____

Shore Excursions:

_____
_____
_____
_____
_____

Items of Interest:

_____
_____
_____
_____
_____
_____
_____
_____
_____
_____

Expenditures:

_____
_____
_____
_____
_____

Daily Cruise Log

Date: _____ Location: _____

Destination Port: _____

Weather: _____

Route: _____

Miles Traveled: _____

Shore Excursions:

_____

_____

_____

_____

_____

Items of Interest:

_____

_____

_____

_____

_____

_____

_____

_____

_____

_____

_____

Expenditures:

_____

_____

_____

_____

_____

_____

Daily Cruise Log

Date: _____ Location: _____

Destination Port: _____

Weather: _____

Route: _____

Miles Traveled: _____

Shore Excursions:

_____

_____

_____

_____

_____

Items of Interest:

_____

_____

_____

_____

_____

_____

_____

_____

_____

_____

Expenditures:

_____

_____

_____

_____

_____

_____

Daily Cruise Log

Date: _____ Location: _____

Destination Port: _____

Weather: _____

Route: _____

Miles Traveled: _____

Shore Excursions:

_____

_____

_____

_____

_____

Items of Interest:

_____

_____

_____

_____

_____

_____

_____

_____

_____

_____

_____

Expenditures:

_____

_____

_____

_____

_____

_____

Daily Cruise Log

Date: _____ Location: _____

Destination Port: _____

Weather: _____

Route: _____

Miles Traveled: _____

Shore Excursions:

_____

_____

_____

_____

_____

Items of Interest:

_____

_____

_____

_____

_____

_____

_____

_____

_____

_____

_____

Expenditures:

_____

_____

_____

_____

_____

_____

Daily Cruise Log

Date: _____ Location: _____

Destination Port: _____

Weather: _____

Route: _____

Miles Traveled: _____

Shore Excursions:

_____

_____

_____

_____

_____

Items of Interest:

_____

_____

_____

_____

_____

_____

_____

_____

_____

_____

_____

Expenditures:

_____

_____

_____

_____

_____

_____

Daily Cruise Log

Date: _____ Location: _____

Destination Port: _____

Weather: _____

Route: _____

Miles Traveled: _____

Shore Excursions:

_____

_____

_____

_____

_____

Items of Interest:

_____

_____

_____

_____

_____

_____

_____

_____

_____

_____

_____

Expenditures:

_____

_____

_____

_____

_____

_____

Daily Cruise Log

Date: _____ Location: _____

Destination Port: _____

Weather: _____

Route: _____

Miles Traveled: _____

Shore Excursions:

_____

_____

_____

_____

_____

Items of Interest:

_____

_____

_____

_____

_____

_____

_____

_____

_____

_____

_____

Expenditures:

_____

_____

_____

_____

_____

_____

Daily Cruise Log

Date: _____ Location: _____

Destination Port: _____

Weather: _____

Route: _____

Miles Traveled: _____

Shore Excursions:

_____
_____
_____
_____
_____

Items of Interest:

_____
_____
_____
_____
_____
_____
_____
_____
_____
_____
_____

Expenditures:

_____
_____
_____
_____
_____
_____

Daily Cruise Log

Date: _____ Location: _____

Destination Port: _____

Weather: _____

Route: _____

Miles Traveled: _____

Shore Excursions:

_____

_____

_____

_____

_____

Items of Interest:

_____

_____

_____

_____

_____

_____

_____

_____

_____

_____

_____

Expenditures:

_____

_____

_____

_____

_____

_____

Daily Cruise Log

Date: _____ Location: _____

Destination Port: _____

Weather: _____

Route: _____

Miles Traveled: _____

Shore Excursions:

_____

_____

_____

_____

_____

Items of Interest:

_____

_____

_____

_____

_____

_____

_____

_____

_____

_____

Expenditures:

_____

_____

_____

_____

_____

_____

Daily Cruise Log

Date: _____ Location: _____

Destination Port: _____

Weather: _____

Route: _____

Miles Traveled: _____

Shore Excursions:

_____
_____
_____
_____
_____

Items of Interest:

_____
_____
_____
_____
_____
_____
_____
_____
_____
_____
_____

Expenditures:

_____
_____
_____
_____
_____

Daily Cruise Log

Date: _____ Location: _____

Destination Port: _____

Weather: _____

Route: _____

Miles Traveled: _____

Shore Excursions:

_____

_____

_____

_____

_____

Items of Interest:

_____

_____

_____

_____

_____

_____

_____

_____

_____

_____

Expenditures:

_____

_____

_____

_____

_____

_____

Daily Cruise Log

Date: _____ Location: _____

Destination Port: _____

Weather: _____

Route: _____

Miles Traveled: _____

Shore Excursions:

_____

_____

_____

_____

_____

Items of Interest:

_____

_____

_____

_____

_____

_____

_____

_____

_____

_____

_____

Expenditures:

_____

_____

_____

_____

_____

_____

Daily Cruise Log

Date: _____ Location: _____

Destination Port: _____

Weather: _____

Route: _____

Miles Traveled: _____

Shore Excursions:

_____

_____

_____

_____

_____

Items of Interest:

_____

_____

_____

_____

_____

_____

_____

_____

_____

_____

_____

Expenditures:

_____

_____

_____

_____

_____

_____

Daily Cruise Log

Date: _____ Location: _____

Destination Port: _____

Weather: _____

Route: _____

Miles Traveled: _____

Shore Excursions:

_____

_____

_____

_____

_____

Items of Interest:

_____

_____

_____

_____

_____

_____

_____

_____

_____

_____

_____

Expenditures:

_____

_____

_____

_____

_____

_____

Daily Cruise Log

Date: _____ Location: _____

Destination Port: _____

Weather: _____

Route: _____

Miles Traveled: _____

Shore Excursions:

_____
_____
_____
_____
_____

Items of Interest:

_____
_____
_____
_____
_____
_____
_____
_____
_____
_____
_____

Expenditures:

_____
_____
_____
_____
_____
_____

Daily Cruise Log

Date: _____ Location: _____

Destination Port: _____

Weather: _____

Route: _____

Miles Traveled: _____

Shore Excursions:

_____

_____

_____

_____

_____

Items of Interest:

_____

_____

_____

_____

_____

_____

_____

_____

_____

_____

_____

Expenditures:

_____

_____

_____

_____

_____

Daily Cruise Log

Date: _____ Location: _____

Destination Port: _____

Weather: _____

Route: _____

Miles Traveled: _____

Shore Excursions:

_____

_____

_____

_____

_____

Items of Interest:

_____

_____

_____

_____

_____

_____

_____

_____

_____

_____

Expenditures:

_____

_____

_____

_____

_____

_____

Daily Cruise Log

Date: _____ Location: _____

Destination Port: _____

Weather: _____

Route: _____

Miles Traveled: _____

Shore Excursions:

_____

_____

_____

_____

_____

Items of Interest:

_____

_____

_____

_____

_____

_____

_____

_____

_____

_____

_____

Expenditures:

_____

_____

_____

_____

_____

_____

Daily Cruise Log

Date: _____ Location: _____

Destination Port: _____

Weather: _____

Route: _____

Miles Traveled: _____

Shore Excursions:

_____

_____

_____

_____

_____

Items of Interest:

_____

_____

_____

_____

_____

_____

_____

_____

_____

_____

_____

Expenditures:

_____

_____

_____

_____

_____

_____

Daily Cruise Log

Date: _____ Location: _____

Destination Port: _____

Weather: _____

Route: _____

Miles Traveled: _____

Shore Excursions:

_____

_____

_____

_____

_____

Items of Interest:

_____

_____

_____

_____

_____

_____

_____

_____

_____

_____

_____

Expenditures:

_____

_____

_____

_____

_____

_____

Daily Cruise Log

Date: _____ Location: _____

Destination Port: _____

Weather: _____

Route: _____

Miles Traveled: _____

Shore Excursions:

_____
_____
_____
_____
_____

Items of Interest:

_____
_____
_____
_____
_____
_____
_____
_____
_____
_____
_____

Expenditures:

_____
_____
_____
_____
_____
_____

Daily Cruise Log

Date: _____ Location: _____

Destination Port: _____

Weather: _____

Route: _____

Miles Traveled: _____

Shore Excursions:

_____

_____

_____

_____

_____

Items of Interest:

_____

_____

_____

_____

_____

_____

_____

_____

_____

_____

_____

Expenditures:

_____

_____

_____

_____

_____

_____

Daily Cruise Log

Date: _____ Location: _____

Destination Port: _____

Weather: _____

Route: _____

Miles Traveled: _____

Shore Excursions:

_____

_____

_____

_____

_____

Items of Interest:

_____

_____

_____

_____

_____

_____

_____

_____

_____

_____

_____

Expenditures:

_____

_____

_____

_____

_____

Daily Cruise Log

Date: _____ Location: _____

Destination Port: _____

Weather: _____

Route: _____

Miles Traveled: _____

Shore Excursions:

_____
_____
_____
_____
_____

Items of Interest:

_____
_____
_____
_____
_____
_____
_____
_____
_____
_____
_____

Expenditures:

_____
_____
_____
_____
_____
_____

Daily Cruise Log

Date: _____ Location: _____

Destination Port: _____

Weather: _____

Route: _____

Miles Traveled: _____

Shore Excursions:

_____

_____

_____

_____

_____

Items of Interest:

_____

_____

_____

_____

_____

_____

_____

_____

_____

_____

Expenditures:

_____

_____

_____

_____

_____

_____

Daily Cruise Log

Date: _____ Location: _____

Destination Port: _____

Weather: _____

Route: _____

Miles Traveled: _____

Shore Excursions:

_____
_____
_____
_____
_____

Items of Interest:

_____
_____
_____
_____
_____
_____
_____
_____
_____
_____
_____

Expenditures:

_____
_____
_____
_____
_____
_____

Daily Cruise Log

Date: _____ Location: _____

Destination Port: _____

Weather: _____

Route: _____

Miles Traveled: _____

Shore Excursions:

_____
_____
_____
_____
_____

Items of Interest:

_____
_____
_____
_____
_____
_____
_____
_____
_____
_____
_____

Expenditures:

_____
_____
_____
_____
_____
_____

Daily Cruise Log

Date: _____ Location: _____

Destination Port: _____

Weather: _____

Route: _____

Miles Traveled: _____

Shore Excursions:

_____

_____

_____

_____

_____

Items of Interest:

_____

_____

_____

_____

_____

_____

_____

_____

_____

_____

_____

Expenditures:

_____

_____

_____

_____

_____

_____

Daily Cruise Log

Date: _____ Location: _____

Destination Port: _____

Weather: _____

Route: _____

Miles Traveled: _____

Shore Excursions:

_____

_____

_____

_____

_____

Items of Interest:

_____

_____

_____

_____

_____

_____

_____

_____

_____

_____

_____

Expenditures:

_____

_____

_____

_____

_____

_____

Daily Cruise Log

Date: _____ Location: _____

Destination Port: _____

Weather: _____

Route: _____

Miles Traveled: _____

Shore Excursions:

_____

_____

_____

_____

_____

Items of Interest:

_____

_____

_____

_____

_____

_____

_____

_____

_____

_____

_____

Expenditures:

_____

_____

_____

_____

_____

_____

Daily Cruise Log

Date: _____ Location: _____

Destination Port: _____

Weather: _____

Route: _____

Miles Traveled: _____

Shore Excursions:

_____
_____
_____
_____
_____

Items of Interest:

_____
_____
_____
_____
_____
_____
_____
_____
_____
_____
_____

Expenditures:

_____
_____
_____
_____
_____
_____

Daily Cruise Log

Date: _____ Location: _____

Destination Port: _____

Weather: _____

Route: _____

Miles Traveled: _____

Shore Excursions:

_____

_____

_____

_____

_____

Items of Interest:

_____

_____

_____

_____

_____

_____

_____

_____

_____

_____

_____

Expenditures:

_____

_____

_____

_____

_____

_____

Daily Cruise Log

Date: _____ Location: _____

Destination Port: _____

Weather: _____

Route: _____

Miles Traveled: _____

Shore Excursions:

_____

_____

_____

_____

_____

Items of Interest:

_____

_____

_____

_____

_____

_____

_____

_____

_____

_____

_____

Expenditures:

_____

_____

_____

_____

_____

_____

Daily Cruise Log

Date: _____ Location: _____

Destination Port: _____

Weather: _____

Route: _____

Miles Traveled: _____

Shore Excursions:

_____

_____

_____

_____

_____

Items of Interest:

_____

_____

_____

_____

_____

_____

_____

_____

_____

_____

_____

Expenditures:

_____

_____

_____

_____

_____

_____

CONGRATULATIONS!

You finished your journal. You are now an Author!

Do you know you can turn this journal into a book?

To help you make your journal, and anything else you may have written, into a real, live book, I have created a book which shows you how.

It's Fun, Easy, and Rewarding, and you can even get away with a typo now and then.
Best of all, it doesn't have to cost you a cent!

This book tells you how. You can find it at Amazon.com and other retailers.

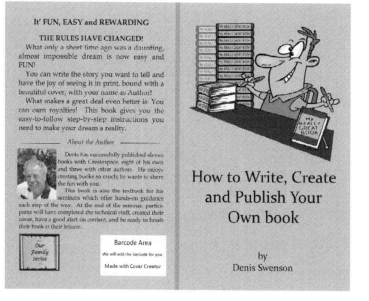

It' FUN, EASY and REWARDING

THE RULES HAVE CHANGED!
What only a short time ago was a daunting, almost impossible dream is now easy and FUN!
You can write the story you want to tell and have the joy of seeing it in print, bound with a beautiful cover, with your name as Author!
What makes a great deal even better is: You can earn royalties! This book gives you the easy-to-follow step-by-step instructions you need to make your dream a reality.

───── About the Author ─────

Denis has successfully published eleven books with Createspace, eight of his own and three with other authors. He enjoys creating books so much; he wants to share the fun with you.
This book is also the textbook for his seminars which offer hands-on guidance each step of the way. At the end of the seminar, participants will have completed the technical stuff, created their cover, have a good start on content, and be ready to finish their book at their leisure.

Our Family Series

Barcode Area
We will add the barcode for you
Made with Cover Creator

How to Write, Create and Publish Your Own book

by
Denis Swenson

About the Authors

Denis and Deanne love to travel and they love to record their journeys. To make record keeping easier and more fun, they created their own Travel Journals for the notes they jot down along the way. Ideas for books come from everywhere, and their journals make it easier to remember details, names and places, when they are back home, making photo books, and incorporating what they learned into their novels.

Denis writes historical fiction, (he calls it "Ancestral Fiction") because he uses his ancestors as characters in the novels. He has made a game of it by asking himself what ancestor may have visited every place he travels to and under what circumstances. His intensive research into family history has revealed how much our ancestors traveled in their lifetime. Many of our European ancestors journeyed far and wide as ordinary sailors or soldiers and yet all we know about them is, "Oh, my ancestors lived in France." While that may certainly be true, it doesn't mean they never left the farm.

Deanne writes in several genres. When she writes romance she often, as in the case of "Boogie Boarding Blues", (which is set in Hawaii where the authors lived for ten years), makes the story into a travel guide. She also has written "How to be a Manager and Love it! Work Relationships that Work." And, she has a true crime book coming out in early 2015 titled, "The Baby Snatcher".

New ideas come to them as they travel and ideas not written down can be easily lost, especially if the book the idea sparks isn't written for years.

Denis is writing a thirty-three book series called the 'Our Family Series' which records family history beginning with Adam and Eve and continuing down to his great-grandchild. It is not unusual for him to imagine his ancestor, Antoine Beaudry, fighting pirates in the Caribbean while the author is exploring the islands on a cruise ship.

Antoine's adventures will have to wait until fifteen more books are written in chronological order, but notes recorded in the journal will be put to good use when the novel is finally underway.

Other Books by Denis Swenson

Available for Kindle and in print from Amazon.com and other retailers:

Adam and Eve

The Adam Scrolls

Noah

The Gathering of the Clan

The Voyageur

Lee Hart
Book One: The Early Years

Lee and Tonaria
Book Two: A Uniquely Western Relationship

Visit www.ourfamilyseries.com for links to buy books, news of future books as they become available, a list of the thirty-three books written and proposed for the series, and to email the authors with any questions or comments.

Other Books by Deanne Swenson

Available for Kindle and in print from Amazon.com
and other retailers:

How to be a Manager
And Love it

Boogie Boarding Blues

Baby Snatcher

Travel Journals, (Several to choose from)

Visit www.ourfamilyseries.com for links to buy
books, news of future books as they become
available, a list of the thirty-three books written and
proposed for the series, and to email the authors with
any questions or comments.

If you liked the book, please consider leaving a review.
It's a huge help to both authors and readers.

Thank you!

You may also reach me on my email at
deanneswenson@yahoo.com.

46702416R00063

Printed in Poland
by Amazon Fulfillment
Poland Sp. z o.o., Wrocław